First World War
and Army of Occupation
War Diary
France, Belgium and Germany

51 DIVISION
Divisional Troops
Divisional Trench Mortar Batteries
1 August 1916 - 30 November 1918

WO95/2854/7

The Naval & Military Press Ltd
www.nmarchive.com
Published in association with The National Archives

Published by

The Naval & Military Press Ltd

Unit 10 Ridgewood Industrial Park,

Uckfield, East Sussex,

TN22 5QE England

Tel: +44 (0) 1825 749494

www.naval-military-press.com

www.nmarchive.com

This diary has been reprinted in facsimile from the original. Any imperfections are inevitably reproduced and the quality may fall short of modern type and cartographic standards.

© Crown Copyright
Images reproduced by permission of The National Archives, London, England, 2015.

Contents

Document type	Place/Title	Date From	Date To
Heading	WO95/2854/7 (51 Divn) Divnl. Trench Mortar Bty 1916 Aug-1918 Nov		
Heading	51st Division Divl Trench Mortar Btys Aug 1916-Nov 1918		
Heading	51st Divisional Artillery. 51st Divisional Trench Mortars August 1916		
War Diary	High Wood	01/08/1916	08/08/1916
War Diary	Vivier Mill	09/08/1916	11/08/1916
War Diary	Bonnay	12/08/1916	14/08/1916
War Diary	Lynde	14/08/1916	16/08/1916
War Diary	Armentieres	17/08/1916	31/08/1916
Operation(al) Order(s)	Operation Order. Trench Mortar Batteries Appendix 1A	24/08/1916	24/08/1916
Miscellaneous	O.C., 51/X T.M. Battery Appendix 1	16/08/1916	16/08/1916
Operation(al) Order(s)	51st Division Artillery Operation Order No. 47. Appendix 2	28/08/1916	28/08/1916
Miscellaneous	Artillery Action in Connection With Discharge of Gas.		
Miscellaneous	51st D.A. No. B.M. 96/3 Appendix 3	30/08/1916	30/08/1916
Heading	51st Division Medium & Heavy Trench Mortar War Diary 1/9/16 to 30/9/16 Vol 2		
War Diary	Armentieres	01/09/1916	25/09/1916
War Diary	Fletre	25/09/1916	30/09/1916
Operation(al) Order(s)	Operation Order No. 2.	03/09/1916	03/09/1916
Operation(al) Order(s)	Operation Order No. 7 for Bombardments By 2" Trench Mortars. on the 13th 14th & 15th Sept 1916. Appendix II		
Miscellaneous	Fire Scheme For 2" TM's in Conjunction With Raid By Ref Map "Bois Grenier" Appendix III		
Miscellaneous	Fire Scheme For 2" TM's No. 10 in Conjunction With Raid By Appendix V		
Miscellaneous	Fire Scheme No. 9 For 2" TM's in Conjunction With Raid By Ref. Map "Houplines" Appendix IV		
Miscellaneous	Fire Scheme No. 5 For 2"+3" TM's To Take Place on Night of 16th /17th in Conjunction With Raid By Ref. Map. Bois Grenier Appendix IV		
Heading	War Diary of 51st Division Trench Mortars From 1 October 1916 to 31st October 1916 Vol III		
War Diary	Fletre	01/10/1916	01/10/1916
War Diary	Doullens	01/10/1916	01/10/1916
War Diary	Authieule	02/10/1916	03/10/1916
War Diary	Bus. Les. Artois.	04/10/1916	07/10/1916
War Diary	Hebuterne	08/10/1916	31/10/1916
Heading	War Diary of 51st Divisional Trench Mortar Batteries. From 1st November to 30th November 1916. Vol 4		
War Diary	Thievres & Sailly Au Bois	01/11/1916	14/11/1916
War Diary	Thievres	14/11/1916	24/11/1916
War Diary	Bouzincourt	24/11/1916	30/11/1916
Heading	War Diary Trench Mortar Batteries 51st (H). Division From 1st December, 1916 To 31st December, 1916 Vol 4		
War Diary	Bouzincourt.	01/12/1916	31/12/1916

Heading	War Diary 51st Divisional Trench Mortars From 1st January 1917 to 31/1/17. Vol 6		
War Diary	Bouzincourt	01/01/1917	06/01/1917
War Diary	Hevre	06/01/1917	31/01/1917
Heading	War Diary for 1st February 1917 to 28th February 1917. Trench Mortar Batteries. Vol 7.		
War Diary	L'Heure	01/02/1917	28/02/1917
War Diary	War Diary From 1st March 1917 to 31st March 1917 of 51/V.X.Y.Z. Trench Mortar Batteries Vol 8.		
War Diary	In The Field	01/03/1917	31/03/1917
War Diary	In The Field	15/03/1917	21/03/1917
Heading	51st Division T.M. Bttys April 1917. X.Y.Z.V.		
Heading	51st Division Trench Mortar War Diary From 1st April 1917 to 30th April 1917 Vol 9		
War Diary	With 51st Div in the line between A 22d 20.85 and A30a 15.15.	01/04/1917	10/04/1917
Heading	War Diary From 1st May 1917 To 31st May 1917 51st Division T.M. Batteries Vol 10.		
War Diary	In The Field	01/05/1917	31/05/1917
Heading	Trench Mortars 51" Divisional Artillery War Diary From 1st June 1917 to 30th June 1917 Vol XI		
War Diary	In The Field	01/06/1917	30/06/1917
Heading	Trench Mortars War Diary From 1.7.17 To 31.7.17 Vol 12		
War Diary	In The Field	01/07/1917	31/07/1917
Heading	51th D.A. Trench Mortars War Diary From 1.8.17 to 31.8.17. Vol 13.		
War Diary	In the Field	01/08/1917	30/08/1917
Heading	War Diary From 1st Sept 1917 to 30th Sept 1917 Of 51 Div Artillery Trench Mortar Batteries Vol 14		
War Diary	In The Field	01/09/1917	30/09/1917
Heading	War Diary From 1/10/17 to 31/10/17 of 51st (H) Div. Trench Mortar Batteries Vol 15.		
War Diary	In The Field	01/10/1917	31/10/1917
Heading	War Diary From 1/11/17 to 30/11/17 51 Div Arty Trench Mortar Batters. Vol 16.		
War Diary	In The Field	01/11/1917	30/11/1917
Heading	War Diary From 1/12/17 To 31/12/17. 51st (H) Div. T.M. Batteries. Vol 17. 21 (A)		
War Diary	In The Field	01/12/1917	31/12/1917
Heading	War Diary From 1.1.18. To 31.1.18. of 51st Div. Artillery T.M. Batteries Vol 18.		
War Diary	In The Field	01/01/1918	31/01/1918
Heading	War Diary From 1st Feb. 1918 To 28th Feb. 1918 of 51st (H) Div. Artillery T.M. Batteries Vol 19		
War Diary	In The Field	01/02/1918	28/02/1918
Heading	War Diary From 1/3/18. To 31/3/18. 51 T.M.B.S. Vol 20.		
War Diary	Field	01/03/1918	31/03/1918
Heading	51st Divisional Artillery War Diary D.T.M.O. 51st Divisional Artillery April 1918.		
War Diary	Field	01/04/1918	30/04/1918
Heading	War Diary of 51st Div Arty T.M. Batts For May. 1918 Vol 22		
War Diary	Field	01/05/1918	31/05/1918

Heading	War Diary of 51st Div. Art. T.M. Batteries For June 1918. Vol 23.		
War Diary	Field	01/06/1918	30/06/1918
Heading	Divisional Artillery 51st (Highland) Division 51st Trench Mortar Battery July. 1918		
War Diary	Field	01/07/1918	31/07/1918
Heading	War Diary From 1st Aug. 1918 to 31st Aug. 1918. of 51st Div. I.M. Batts Vol 25.		
War Diary	Field	01/08/1918	31/08/1918
Heading	War Diary From 1st Sept. 1918 to 30th Sept. 1918. 51 T.M.B. Vol 26.		
War Diary	Field	01/09/1918	30/09/1918
Heading	War Diary From 1st Oct. 1918 To 31st Oct. 1918. 51st T.M. Batteries Vol 27.		
War Diary	Field	01/10/1918	31/10/1918
Miscellaneous	153rd Trench Mortar Battery. Narrative of Operations Period 11/12 Oct-28/29 Oct.	06/11/1918	06/11/1918
Heading	War Diary From 1st Nov. to 30th Nov. 1918 51D T.M. Bty. Vol 28.		
War Diary	Field	01/11/1918	30/11/1918

WO 95 2854/7

(51 Divn) Divnl. Trench Mortar Bty

1916 Aug – 1918 Nov

51ST DIVISION

DIVL TRENCH MORTAR BTYS
AUG 1916-NOV 1918

51ST DIVISION

51st. Divisional Artillery.

51st DIVISIONAL TRENCH MORTARS

AUGUST 1 9 1 6::::

WAR DIARY
or
INTELLIGENCE SUMMARY.
(Erase heading not required.)

Army Form C. 2118.

CONFIDENTIAL
No 31 (A)
HIGHLAND DIVISION

Instructions regarding War Diaries and Intelligence Summaries are contained in F. S. Regs., Part II. and the Staff Manual respectively. Title pages will be prepared in manuscript.

Place	Date	Hour	Summary of Events and Information	Remarks and references to Appendices
HIGH WOOD	1/8/16 to 6/8/16		The section of 51/X Trench Mortar Battery in action. 51/1 & 51/2 Batteries in Rest billets until 153rd & 154th Infantry Bryn. has reoccupied 1st MAMETZ Wood MEAULTE	R/34
	7/8/16		51/X Battery relieved by a battery of 33rd Division and marched to Buire with 153rd Infantry Brigade at DERNANCOURT.	R/34
	8/8/16	9 am	Marched to join 51st D.A.C. at VIVIER MILL when 51/X 51/Y & 51/2 Batteries concentrated	R/34
VIVIER MILL	9/8/16 10/8/16		at VIVIER MILL	R/34
	11/8/16	10 am	Batteries moved out Divisional Artillery & Bivouacs at BONNAY	R/34
BONNAY	12/8/16 13/8/16		at BONNAY	R/34
	14/8/16	10 am	Batteries moved by Motor Lorry to entraining stations 51/X & 51/Y to LONGEAUX & 51/2 to SALEVX Station. Entraining there for THIENNES & ARQUES respectively. arriving at their stations night of 14/15th	R/34
LYNDE	14/8/16		Rejoined 51st DAC at LYNDE	R/34
LYNDE	15/8/16	2 pm	Moved off their area and took over from NZ/X D/Z/Y & NZ/Z TM Btys positions E of ARMENTIERES	Appendix I R/34
ARMENTIERES	17/8/16 to 22/8/16		Batteries in action. Very little firing being carried out owing to Infantry only Berks in our Front Line. One enemy Machine Gun Emplacement was destroyed by 51/Y TM Batty on night 22/8/16	R/34 R/34

Army Form C. 2118.

WAR DIARY
or
INTELLIGENCE SUMMARY.

(Erase heading not required.)

Instructions regarding War Diaries and Intelligence Summaries are contained in F. S. Regs., Part II. and the Staff Manual respectively. Title pages will be prepared in manuscript.

Place	Date	Hour	Summary of Events and Information	Remarks and references to Appendices
ARMENTIERES	25/8/16		Batteries still in Line. Firing still limited owing to Infantry working parties	RMR
	26/8/16	2pm	51/2 T.M Battery withdrew from the line in accordance with instructions received from CRA and	RMR. Appendix 1A.
	27/8/16	—	51/X and 51/Y TM Batteries took up new position to cover front from as possible. 51/X & 51/Y in action. 51/2 in Rest billets.	RMR
	28/8/16	4pm	51/2 moved into the line with 1 mortar & Registered on Enemy Line. 51/X & 51/Y took up temporary position & Registered on Enemy Front line & bore along the front held by Division in accordance with O.O. No 47. of 28/8/16. Total flare & night of 29-30th	RMR. Appendix 2
	29/8/16	9pm	hand refusable for gas attack & that on happened. Bomb Store in Enemy front line was blown up by direct hit from 51/4 Battery	RMR
	30/8/16	12.30pm	Orders received to concentrate 2 Batteries Stokes in left sector, to cut wire. Wire & shelters of line mg & mortars were got untraceable one got but went out of action during Registration	
	31/8/16 1.10pm		Trench Mortars opened fire on Enemy line & fired till 7=7 am. after discharge of gas in accordance with 51st D.A BM 96/3	RMR. Appendix 3

[signature] Capt.
OOTh 51st Division

Operation Order.
Trench Mortar Batteries

Appendix 1A

Secret.

Ref map. Houplines & Bois Grenier.
Scale 1/10.000.

On the relief of 154 Inf. Bde. 51/Z T.M. Batty. will withdraw to Billets in Armentieres, taking One Gun & One Bed.

51/Y T.M. Batty will take over the sector at present occupied by 51/Z, also two Guns complete & all spare Beds, viz 5 Beds. The Guns for 51/Y T.M. Batty should be re-distributed in the available positions to cover as far as possible the Front held by Inf. Bde. Left Sector.

51/X Batty will take over 2 Guns complete from 51/Y & will re-distribute the Guns in available positions to cover Front held by Inf. Bde. Right Sector

The spare Beds belonging to 51/Z should be stored in a position under cover, say C28d 80.60, central to both X & Y Batteries so that they will be available for any special purpose if required.

The opportunity should be taken to re-arrange Ammunition so that each Store will contain complete rounds & all surplus component parts returned to Stores Lue.

RB Life Capt.
D.O.T.M.

24.8.16.

Issued at 4 pm.

Note Battery officers (in Trenches) should meet at Hqrs of 51/Y Japan Road. at 12 noon 25.8.16.

SECRET

Appendix 1

O.C.,
   51/X T.M. Battery ✓
   51/Y - do -
   51/Z - do -

Batteries will proceed to the front area by motor bus leaving Headquarters, D.A.C., at 2 p.m., on 16th inst., and will take over from New Zealand Division night 16th/17th. Relief to be completed by 5 p.m., on 17th inst. Guides will meet Batteries at Headquarters N.Z. Divisional Artillery.

51/X T.M. Battery will take over 2 Mortars and 2 extra pairs wheels complete with stores and will hand over same number to out-going Battery.

51/Y and 51/Z T.M. Batteries will each take over 4 Mortars complete and hand over the same number to out-going Battery.

All additional stores over and above those laid down in Mobilization Store Tables also telephones will be retained by Batteries. 21 hand carts will be taken over.

51/X T.M. Battery will leave behind 1 officer to hand over to N.Z. Division.

Battery Commanders will report to D.O.T.M., 51st Division when relief has been completed.

Rations for consumption on 17th inst will be carried out with the Batteries.

                                                Captain,
16/8/16.   D.O.T.M., 51st Division.

SECRET
****

51st DIVISIONAL ARTILLERY
OPERATION ORDER No.47

Appendix 3

COPY No. 17

Reference Maps
HOUPLINES 1/10,000
BOIS GRENIER 1/10,000

28th August, 1916.

1. Gas will be discharged on the front of the 153rd Infantry Brigade during the night 29th/30th, or on the first night after that date when suitable conditions obtain.

2. The gas discharge will be accompanied by -

   (a) M.G. fire to cover the sound of emission of gas.

   (b) Smoke discharge in the intervals between the gas emplacements.

   (c) Artillery and T.M. bombardment.

3. Programme of Artillery bombardment is attached.

4. The general time table of the operation is as follows :-

-24 mins to -19 mins	1st burst of M.G. fire.
-3 mins to +2 mins	2nd burst of M.G. fire
0	Discharge
0 +4	Smoke candles in intervals between emplacements.
0 +4	Artillery and T.M. bombardment
0 +15	Rogers and Smoke Candles cease
0 +20	Artillery and T.M. bombardment ceases

The zero hour will be notified later.

5. Acknowledge

Issued at 4.30 p.m.

                                           Major R.A.,
                                   Brigade Major,
                            51st Divisional Artillery.

Copy No.	
1 - 5	Right Group
6 + 11	Left Group
12	256th Brigade R.F.A.
13 - 14	51st Division "G"
15	2nd Anzac R.A.
16	153rd Infantry Brigade
17	D.T.M.O.
18	Diary
19	Office.

SECRET.
****

ARTILLERY ACTION IN CONNECTION WITH DISCHARGE OF GAS

TIME.	UNIT.	ROUNDS.	OBJECTIVE.
1st PHASE.			
0+4 mins to 0+11 mins	A/256	75-A, 75-AX	Trench from I.5b.2.8 to C.29c.8.4
	B/256	75-A, 75-AX	Trench from C.29c.8.4 to C.29a.4.1
	One gun		
	A/260	30-A	Enfilade trench C.29c.4.9 to C.29d.1.2
	D/255	56-BX	Front system of trenches from C.29d.1.2 to C.29c.4.9
	C/256	75-A, 75-AX	Trench from C.23c.9.1 to C.23c. 8.7
	D/255	75-A, 75-AX	Trench from C.23c.8.7 to C.23b. 15.35
	B/256	56-BX	Front system of trenches from C.23c.9.3 to C.23b.1.2
	B/260	75-A, 75-AX	Trench from C.17d.1.0 to C.17c.9.5
	A/260	50-A, 50-AX	Trench from C.17c.9.5 to C.17c.7.9
	" (4 guns)	30-A	Enfilade trench from C.17c.7.9 to C.17d.0.3
	" (1 gun)		
	D/260	56-BX	Front system of trenches from C.17d.0.3 to C.17c.7.9
2nd PHASE.			
0+11 mins to 0+17 mins	A/256	60-A, 60-AX	Trench from I.5b.4.0 to I.5b.2.8
	B/256	60-A, 60-AX	Trench from C.29c.9.6 to C.29b.0.2 and from C.29c.6.9 to C.29a.8.3
	one gun		
	A/260	25-A	Trench from C.29a.55.40 to C.29.c.9.7
	D/255	50-BX	Trench from C.29d.5.1 to C.29d.6.6
	C/256	60-A, 60-AX	Trench from C.29a.6.4 to C.23c.9.1
	D/255	60-A, 60-AX	Trench from C.23d.15.50 to C.23b.3.2
	B/256	50-BX	LES 4 HALLOTS FME and trenches round it
	B/260	60-A, 60-AX	Trench from C.23b. 1.4 to C.17d. 1.0
	A/260 (4 guns)	45-A, 45-AX	Trench from C.17c.7.9 to C.17a. 9.3
	" (1 gun)	25-A	Enfilade trench from C.17a.2.6 to U.17 Central
	D/260	50-BX	Trench from C.17d.4.0 to C.17 Central

- 2 -

TIME.	UNIT.	ROUNDS.	OBJECTIVE.
3rd PHASE.			
0 + 17 mins) to) 0 + 20 mins)	Same as 1st Phase.	Per Battery 18-Pounders 28-A, 26-X. 4.5" Hows. 20-X.	Same as 1st Phase.

At 0 + 1 hour 30 minutes and at 0 + 2 hours 15 minutes each Battery will fire 2 rounds gun fire at the targets for 1st Phase.

Appendix 3

SECRET.

Right Group
Left Group
256th Brigade R.F.A.   )
51st Division "G".   )   51st D.A. No. B.M.96/3
R.A. IInd ANZAC Corps.   ) For information
153rd Infantry Brigade.   )
D.T.M.O.   )

Reference Maps:-
    HOUPLINES   1/10,000
    BOIS GRENIER 1/10,000.

1.   The amendment to "Artillery action in connection with discharge of Gas" issued under my number B.M. 96 of 28/8/16 is now cancelled.
        The Artillery action will now be as ordered in the table issued with Operation Order No.47, except that the last two lines of the second page of the table are cancelled.

2.   A second table for Artillery bombardment, in connection with an Infantry raid opposite trenches 86 and 87, is attached.

3.   Both bombardments will take place on the same night after the discharge of gas.

4.   The signal that the raiding party has returned will be 2 rockets discharged together and breaking into golden and silver rain.

5.   The whole general programme will now be as follows:-

        O   Release of gas.

        O plus 4   Artillery bombardment and smoke.

        O plus 20   Artillery bombardment and smoke cease.

        O plus 30   Artillery bombardment on front of raid
                    commences and raiding party form
                    up. - Feint bombardments open on
                    other fronts.

        O plus 37   Raiding party goes in and Artillery
                    lifts to support line and flanks
                    of raid.

6.   Group Commanders will arrange to synchronise watches with G.O.C., 153rd Infantry Brigade.

7.   Acknowledge.

                                        Major R.A.,
                                        Brigade Major,
30th August 1916.   51st Divisional Artillery.

CONFIDENTIAL
No 21/9
HIGHLAND
DIVISION

Confidential

51st Division Medium & Heavy Trench Mortars

Vol 2

WAR DIARY.

1/9/16 to 30/9/16

WAR DIARY
or
INTELLIGENCE SUMMARY.
(Erase heading not required.)

Army Form C. 2118.

Instructions regarding War Diaries and Intelligence Summaries are contained in F.S. Regs., Part II and the Staff Manual respectively. Title pages will be prepared in manuscript.

Place	Date	Hour	Summary of Events and Information	Remarks and references to Appendices
ARMENTIERES	1/9/16 to 8/9/16		51/X & 51/Y T.M. Batteries in the line only ordinary Retaliatory Fire going on.	R54.
	9/9/16		51/Z T.M Battery moved into the line in accordance with Operation order No 2	Appendix I R54.
	10/9/16		51/X/Y/Z in the line. nothing of importance to report.	R54
	11/9/16 12/9/16 13/9/16 14/9/16 15/9/16		All three Batteries bombarded Enemy trenches & wire in accordance with Operation Order No 7. in conjunction with Artillery. Considerable damage being done.	appendix II R54 II.
	15/16		Firing in conjunction with Raids by 152 & 153 Inf. Bdes. in accordance with FireScheme 8 & 9	Appendix III + IV R54
	16/17		Firing in conjunction with Raids by 153 & 154 Inf. Bdes in accordance with FireScheme No 10 & 5	Appendix V + VI R54
			The gunnery of Trench Mortar Batteries during all these raids was excellent & great damage done Enemy Line & Trenches.	R54.
	18/9/16 19/9/16 20/9/16 21st		Ordinary daily firing going on. Preparing position & Registering guns for Infantry Raid	R54 R54 R54
	22/9/16 23/9/16		Batteries 51/X & 51/Y fired 207 Rounds during Raid by 152 Inf. Bde. Batteries 51/Z + 51/X Batteries were Relieved by 2 Batteries of FRANK'S FORCE	R54 R54
	23/9/16		51/Y Battery withdrew from the line.	R54
	24/9/16 25/9/16		In Billets at ARMENTIERES	R54
	2/9/16		Moved to FLETRE in accordance with orders issued by 51 Divisn	R54
FLETRE	to 30/9/16		In Billets in FLETRE.	R54

R.Blake Capt D.T.M. 51 Divisn

Secret.

Operation Order
No. 2.

1. 51/2nd Trench Mortar Battery will move into the line on the left Sector, with 154th Infantry Bde. & take over part of the front at present occupied by 51/Y Trench Mortar Battery.

2. 51/Y Trench Mortar Battery will remain in the line at the tactical disposal of 154th Infantry Bde. & will in the meantime occupy suitable positions in Centre of front as on taking over from V/N.Z. The O.C. Right Section 154th Inf. Bde. will act as sentinel where he covers the Guns of 51/Y Battery Commanders will report to this office when change over is complete.

Issued at 8·0 pm

H.B.M.Jackson
DOTM

Appendix I.

No 5. Appendix II

SECRET.

Operation Order No 7 for Bombardments by 2" TRENCH MORTARS. on the 13th - 14th & 15th Sept 1916.

BOMBT. NO	DATE	TIME	OBJECTIVE	BATTERY	No of ROUNDS	RATE OF FIRE	REMARKS
1	13-9-16	7AM to 7-2AM	I 5b 30-20 to I 5b 25-30	Y	20	GUNFIRE	152-153 v 154 T.M. Batteries will
2	13-9-16	9-10 AM to 9-12AM	C 23c 90-60 to C 23c 90-75	Z	20	"	Co-operate with 51/x
3	13-9-16	12-25 PM to 12-27PM	I 5b 20-70 to I 5b 20-85	Y	20	"	51/Y v 51/Z respectively
4	13-9-16	6-5 PM to 6-7 PM	C 23b 15-20 to C 23b 15-30	Z	20	"	firing 60 rounds
5	13-9-16	9-15 PM to 9-17 PM	I 5c 70-00 to I 5c 80-20	X	20	"	at the same targets
6	14-9-16	8-20 AM to 8-22 AM	I 5d 30-75 to I 5d 40-90	Y	20	"	& at the same times
7	14-9-16	11AM to 11-2AM	C 17a 40-20 to C 17a 20-30	Z	20	"	
8	14-9-16	3-35 PM to 3-37 PM	I 5d 00-45 to I 5d 10-50	X	20	"	
9	14-9-16	11-20 PM to 11-22 PM	C 17d 00-25 to C 17e 90 40	Z	20	"	
10	15-9-16	6-30 AM to 6-32AM	C 29c 80-45 to C 29c 65-55	Y	20	"	
11	15-9-16	2-5 PM to 2-9 PM	I 11c 50-15 and I 11c 50-35	X	32	"	
12	15-9-16	5-40PM to 5-42PM	C 29a 80-80 to C 29a 80-90	Z	20	"	

REF. MAPS - HOUPLINES v BOIS GRENIER

SCALE 1-10000

PLACE & TIME FOR SYNCHRONIZING WATCHES

WILL BE NOTIFIED LATER

[Signature] Capt.
D.O.T.M.

D.O.T.M.
51st (HIGHLAND) DIVISION.
No. RBF 6
Date 11/9/16

Appendix VIII

SECRET FIRE SCHEME FOR 2" TM's IN CONJUNCTION WITH RAID BY 152nd INF. BDE

REF MAP:- "BOIS GRENIER" No 8
SCALE 1:10000

TIME	DATE	BATTERY	OBJECTIVE	RATE OF FIRE	No of RDS	REMARKS
X till	15/16th	51/X 1GUN	I 11 c 65-45	1 Round per	10 to 15	MUSHROOM RAID.
Infantry	night of	51/X 1GUN	I 11 c 70-07	gunfire	10 to 15	
Signal		51/X 1GUN	I 11 c 62-75	1 minute until the infantry	10 to 15	
their		51/X 1GUN	I 11 c 60-90	two in enemy	10 to 15	To fire from S.W
Return		51/Y 1GUN	I 5 c 65-12	trench util	10 to 15	Enfilade
		51/Y 1GUN	I 11 a 80-30	Return Signal	10 to 15	RAILWAY SALIENT.

NOTE:- TIME OF "X" + TIME + PLACE FOR SYNCHRONISING WATCHES
will be notified later by 152 Inf. Brigade

Appendix V

Fire Scheme for 2" T.M's No 10 in Conjunction with Raid by
Ref. Map:- "Houplines"
5th Gordons - 153rd Inf. Bde.
Scale 1:10.000

TIME	DATE	BATTERY	OBJECTIVE	No OF RDS	RATE OF FIRE	REMARKS
X till Inf Signal Return	16/17	51/Z 2 Guns	C17a 30-20 to C17a 40-25	30	Battery 15 secs	
		51/Z 2 Guns	C17c 80-70 & South but on no account N of this point	30	Do Do	

"X" (Time) will be notified later by Inf Bde.

Watches will be Synchronised at Time & Place
to be Notified by 153 Inf. Bde.

Issued at 10-30 a.m.
13/9/16

SECRET   FIRE SCHEME Nº 9. FOR 2" T.M's IN CONJUNCTION WITH RAID BY   Appendix IV

REF. MAP "HOUPLINES"   153rd Infantry Brigade
Scale 1:10,000   7th Black Watch + 7th Gordons

TIME	DATE	BATTERY	OBJECTIVE	RATE OF FIRE	Nº OF Rds	REMARKS.
X tell.	15/10	51/Y 1 Gun	Front Line and Area Round C.29.c.75.45 + 50 yds S.W.	1 Round per Gun per minute with Infantry Signal	10 to 15 10 to 15	Special attention to possible Machine Gun emplacements
Infantry Signal	night of	51/Y 1 Gun				
		51/Z 1 Gun	Front Line and Area Round C.29.a.80.80. 30 yds N + S of this point	Return	10 to 15 10 to 15	
thus		51/Z 1 Gun				
Return		51/Z 1 Gun				

NOTE:- TIME OF X AND TIME AND TRACE FOR SYNCHRONISING WATCHES, ALSO
SIGNAL OF INFANTRY RETURN WILL BE NOTIFIED BY 153RD INF. BDE.

Barrage at H.30 p.m.

Appendix VI

FIRE SCHEME Nos. FOR 2" & 3" T.M's. TO TAKE PLACE ON NIGHT OF 16/17 IN CONJUNCTION WITH RAID BY 9TH BATT. ROYAL SCOTS.

REF. MAP :- "BOIS GRENIER" SCALE 1:10,000

PHASE	BATTERY	OBJECTIVE	No OF RDS	RATE OF FIRE	REMARKS
1ST PHASE X-15 to X-5 mnts	51/Y 4 GUNS	ENEMY WIRE FROM I5c 60.01 to I5c 60.10.	40	BATTERY FIRE 15" SECS.	To be inclined R's "O" RLY. Frontle do
	51/X 4 GUNS		40	"	
	½ 154 4 GUNS	FRONT LINE AT I5c 60.00 to I5c 60.15 AND AREA BEHIND	120	3 RDS PER GUN PER MINUTE.	SPECIAL ATTENTION TO BE PAID To POSSIBLE M.G. EMPLACEMENTS.
	½ 154 4 GUNS.	WIRE + FRONT LINE OF SALIENT FROM I11a 50.30 to I11a 30.12	120	do	BLUFF TO DISTRACT ENEMY ATTENTION
2ND PHASE X-5 to X	51/Y 4 GUNS	AS IN FIRST PHASE	40	GUNFIRE	
	51/X 4 GUNS		40	"	
	½ 154 4 GUNS	AS IN FIRST PHASE	100	NORMAL.	
	½ 154 4 GUNS.		100	"	
3RD PHASE X till INF. SIGNAL RETURN	½ 154 2 GUNS	FRONT LINE I5c 80.20 to I5c 85.25.	40	SLOW	
	½ 154 2 GUNS.	" I11a 60.80 to I11a 60.70	40	"	
	½ 154 4 GUNS.	AS IN FIRST PHASE	40	"	

NOTE :- X (TIME OF) AND TIME + PLACE FOR SYNCHRONISING WATCHES WILL BE NOTIFIED BY 154TH INF. BDE.

THE SIGNAL OF INFANTRY RETURN WILL BE 2 WHITE ROCKETS.

TOTAL 2" AMM" 160 RDS NORMAL TO 180 RD.
3" "STOKES 600 RDS

ISSUED AT :- 3-40 pm 13/9/16.

CONFIDENTIAL.
No 21/A
HIGHLAND DIVISION.

Vol III

Confidential.
War Diary

of

51st Division Trench Mortars.

From 1 October 1916 to 31st October 1916

WAR DIARY or INTELLIGENCE SUMMARY

Army Form C. 2118.

Place	Date	Hour	Summary of Events and Information	Remarks and references to Appendices
FLETRE	1/10/16	1 am.	Reverted to Greenwich Time & left billets to entrain at BAILLEUL for DOULLENS.	
DOULLENS	"	8 am.	Detrained & moved to Bivouacs at AUTHIEULE.	
AUTHIEULE	2/10/16		In Bivouacs	
"	3/10/16	9.30am.	Moved from Bivouacs AUTHIEULE to Bivouacs at BUS-les-ARTOIS arriving there 12 noon.	
BUS-les-ARTOIS	4/10/16 to 6/10/16		In Bivouacs.	
"	7/10/16	8 am.	Moved from BUS-les-ARTOIS to HEBUTERNE. Positions in the line reconnoitred & digging of emplacements commenced	Ref. Map. HEBUTERNE 1/10,000
HEBUTERNE	8/10/16		All Batteries completed emplacements & got mortars in position ready to open fire. Line held from K23B.50.45 to JOHN COPSE.	
"	9/10/16 to 14/10/16		In the line. No firing going on.	
"	15/10/16 to 17/10/16		In same positions. Cutting enemy wire.	
"	17/10/16		51st Division relieved by 31st Division. TM Batteries 51/X, 51/Y & 51/Z remaining under 31st Division.	
"	18/10/16 to 31/10/16		51/X, 51/Y, 51/Z. Still under 31st Division. Personnel of 51/V with 51st D.A.C. employed on Amm^n Dumps.	

H.B.Hife - Capt

Vol 4

CONFIDENTIAL.

WAR DIARY.

of

51st DIVISIONAL TRENCH MORTAR BATTERIES.

From 1st November to 30th November 1916.

WAR DIARY
or
INTELLIGENCE SUMMARY.
(Erase heading not required.)

Army Form C. 2118.

Place	Date	Hour	Summary of Events and Information	Remarks and references to Appendices
THIEVRES & SAILLY AU BOIS	1/11/16 to 14/11/16		51/V T.M. Battery attached to 51st D.A.C. 51/X, 51/Y, 51/Z T.M. Batteries in rest billets.	
THIEVRES.	14/11/16 to 24/11/16		T.M. Batteries 51/X, 51/Y, 51/Z joined 51st D.A.C.	
BOUZINCOURT.	24/11/16 30/11/16		All T.M. Batteries with 51st D.A.C. in billets to date. They moved this date still in billets at BOUZINCOURT.	

Capt. O.O.T.M.
51st Division.

Vol 4

WAR DIARY.

TRENCH MORTAR BATTERIES
51ST (H). DIVISION

From 1st December, 1916.
To. 31st December, 1916.

CONFIDENTIAL
No 27(A) Army Form C. 2118.
HIGHLAND DIVISION.

T.M Batteries, 51st Division

WAR DIARY
or
INTELLIGENCE SUMMARY.
(Erase heading not required.)

Instructions regarding War Diaries and Intelligence Summaries are contained in F. S. Regs., Part II. and the Staff Manual respectively. Title pages will be prepared in manuscript.

Place	Date	Hour	Summary of Events and Information	Remarks and references to Appendices
BOUZINCOURT	1/12/16	—	In Billets.	A/12
	15/12/16			
	29/12/16		Digging at R.F.A. Battery position.	A/12
	8/12/16		No Trench Mortars in action during the period.	
	31/12/16			

A.B. Hunt
O.C. T.M.O. 51st Division

CONFIDENTIAL
No 27(A)
HIGHLAND
DIVISION.

Vol 6

War Diary.

51st Divisional Trench Mortars

From 1st January 1917 to 31/1/17.

CONFIDENTIAL
No 21(?)
HIGHLAND DIVISION.

WAR DIARY
or
INTELLIGENCE SUMMARY.
(Erase heading not required.)

TM Batteries 51st Division

Army Form C. 2118.

Place	Date	Hour	Summary of Events and Information	Remarks and references to Appendices
BOUZINCOURT	1/1/17 to 4/1/17		T M Batteries not in action. Personnel assisting RFA Batts. digging	RA
"	4/1/17		Personnel returned to Billets	ADA
"	4/1/17 to 5/1/17		In Billets	
"	6/1/17		Moved by Motor lorry to L'HEURE	RA
L'HEURE	6/1/17 to 31/1/17		In Rest carrying out Recreational training.	RA

R.D. H?.. Capt.
D.T.M.O. 51st Division

1917

WAR DIARY

1st February 1917 to 28th February 1917.

TRENCH MORTAR BATTERIES.

WAR DIARY

INTELLIGENCE SUMMARY

(Erase heading not required.)

Army Form C. 2118.

Place	Date	Hour	Summary of Events and Information	Remarks and references to Appendices
L'HEURE	1/2/17		51/X 51/Y 51/2 & 51/V Stokes Mortar Batteries undergoing Recreational training & re-equipping. RSM	
	5/2/17		Moved to NOYELLES. RSM	
	6/2/17		" " BOUBERS SUR CANCHE. RSM	
	7/2/17		" " HERNICOURT. RSM	
	8/2/17		" " HOUVELIN. RSM	
	13/2/17		" " ARRAS in Bellols Zone. Personel digging positions for K & L1 Sectors RSM	
	13/2/17 to 29/2/17			
	20/2/17 to 28/2/17		Return Batteries action cutting wire for Raid. Only a small number of Rounds being fired during " RSM	

WB Fitz Capt OJMO

Vol 8

War Diary

from 1st March 1917 to 31st March 1917.

of

51/W.X.Y.Z. Trench Mortar Batteries

WAR DIARY
or
INTELLIGENCE SUMMARY.
(Erase heading not required.)

Army Form C. 2118.

Ref. Trench Map ROCLINCOURT
51B NW. Scale 1/10,000

In the field = 51st Divisional Sector
= From A22d0.9 to A30a2.2

Instructions regarding War Diaries and Intelligence Summaries are contained in F.S. Regs., Part II. and the Staff Manual respectively. Title pages will be prepared in manuscript.

Place	Date	Hour	Summary of Events and Information	Remarks and references to Appendices
In the Trenches	1&2.3.17 to 4.3.17		During this period about 1000 rounds were fired by 51/X, 51/Y + 51/Z T.M. Batteries. These shoots were carried out in 2 places, one with the purpose of a raid and the other to distract attention from the real area.	9.3
Do.	5.3.17	6.9am & 6.39am	237 rounds were fired on flanks of raiding party by 51/X + 51/Y T.M. Battys to draw enemy barrage on wrong direction fired by 51/Z T.M. Batty about 1000 rounds to the S.E. of raid gap to prevent enfilade. Place was made by 1/6 Gordon Hldrs. Map ref. of raid = A30a25.30 to 23d80.10. Raid was successful.	9.2
Do.	6.3.17 to 16.3.17		During this period shoots were cut steadily all along the front line opposite the 51st Division about 2000 rounds in all being fired. The batteries had a most trying time during these 10 days + suffered many casualties.	9.3
Do.	17.3.17	6.41am to 6.58am	Batteries fired 92 Smoke bombs on flanks of raiding party of 118th A + S. Hdrs. @ front of enemy's trenches some casualties occurred whilst firing these smoke bombs. no casualties Raid was carried out on same portion of enemy's trenches as 1/6 Gordons raided on 5th March, 17.	9.3
Do.	18.3.17 to 19.3.17		During this period our batteries were active — cutting the front line + parts of support line were carried out on enemy trenches about 2000 rounds being fired in all.	9.3

Awards + Casualties.

Do.	20.3.17	—	No. 1609 Corporal John Anderson Ramsay R.F.A. attd 51/X T.M. Battery awarded military medal.	9.4 Killed in action 26.3.17 9.5
	Do.	—	No. 83595 Bdr. William James Goulding R.F.A. attd 51/Y T.M. Batty awarded military medal. { Killed in action 5.4.17	9.6
	Do.	—	No. 297 a/Bdr Joseph Pinic 260th Brigade R.F.A. attd 51/Y T.M. Batty awarded military medal.	
	17.3.17	—	No. 61090 Bdr. John Campbell R.F.A. attached Z/51 T.M. Batty. 1 Officer wounded on 30.3.17	9.5
	21.3.17	—	Total casualties during March. 4 O.R. killed – 7 wounded	9.6

Batteries attached to 51st Division during March. 1917.
Y/2 Medium Trench Mortar Battery joined this division on 20th March, 1917. Left to join 34th Division on 31.3.17. 9.4
V/63 Heavy Trench Mortar Battery joined this division on 26th March, 1917. 25

J. Gillespie Capt. DTMO.
51st Divl.

On His Majesty's Service.

51st Division.

T. M. Bttys
April 1917

X X Z Y

51st Division. French Motors. Vol 9

War Diary.

From 1st April 1917. to 30th April 1917.

All the intervening days between 9th + 26th April, 1917 when the tribe was driven to re-sighting guns and generally refitting were spent in front of the line between X/37 T.M Body upwind 37th Division. ARRAS and troops on parade. X/37 T.M Body upwind 37th Division. Army Form C. 2118.

WAR DIARY / INTELLIGENCE SUMMARY
(Erase heading not required)

Instructions regarding War Diaries and Intelligence Summaries are contained in F.S. Regs., Part II. and the Staff Manual respectively. Title pages will be prepared in manuscript.

Ref. 1/1AP
FOLLINCOURT SHEET

Place	Date	Hour	Summary of Events and Information	Remarks and references to Appendices
With 51st Div in the line between A22.d.20.85 and A30a.15.15	1/4/17 to 3/4/17	Occasionally during the day	Bombardment of trenches opposite the Personal Post by medium T.M. batteries of the Division (fire right V/51, V/62 and V/63 Heavy T.M. Battery). Also special wire-cutting by the Middle batteries along enemy front line opposite. 700 rounds of 3" were expended. During this period 600 rounds of 2" trench ammo were expended. On 3/4/17, 1200 rounds of 2" ammo at a dump at A22.d.80.35 (S.E of MONCHEUX) was blown up by enemy artillery fire (5.9" how) and 1 gun totally destroyed. During this firing enemy artillery retaliation whilst we continued to fire, was very heavy. Y/2 medium T.M. batty which went to 34th Division.	21
Do	4/4/17 to 5/4/17	p.m.	Preliminary bombardment before attack commenced. Trench mortars commenced at 6.15 a.m. and continued until the 4th inst. a deliberate steady bombardment with allow trench mortars and 1400 rounds of 3" (Heavy) the 8th inst. During this period 6800 rounds of 2" ammo and front again of bombs opposite the line. Fire on the enemy front line was and front apart were about in this aid were attached to our Division as no Infantry. The Batteries which took part in this were: X, Y + Z/21 and 5" also some also attached to X/51, X/58, X/37 their guns were not kept action with no equipment but the personnel were never reserve and was not called upon to go V/58 was also left into action.	22
			Y/51, Y/58	
			Z/51, Z/58	
			V/51	V/62 V/63
			On the 5th inst. the 2" positions in the FANTOME (A2.d.20.35) were heavily taken on the 5"/9 and 4"/2" two each gun pit had a direct hit and all guns were eliminated only enemy totally destroyed. N.C.O. and 22 were killed while violently showing their guns during this time shelling. Out of 15" medium mortars 1 man were killed while violently showing their guns during this time shelling almost all the same attacked in action on 5th inst. 1 was totally destroyed in the 6 shell. Also on the 6th inst our heavy mortars at A22.d.90.5 were heavily shelled the gun was severely during the 6th inst 24 rounds of ammunition (9".45") and 8 men were killed. On the 6 the 1st 24 rounds of ammunition (9".45") and 8 men were killed. On the 6 the 1st sheet or the 7th inst and another heavy trench mortar bomb during the preliminary shelling of our mortar positions was less than 10 O.R. killed and 9 O.R's wounded. Casualties during preliminary bombardment period were less than 10 O.R. killed and 9 O.R's wounded.	
Do	9/4/17 and 10/4/17		Light mortar batteries engaged in station - during very interesting to see the results of our trench mortar guns his which up a excellent effect. From 11 to 16th into T.M. batteries were engaged in removing their guns from the line to ARRAS and in tidying up ammo dumps and in digging stain guns in shelter also employed for a few days in generally capturing guns (from 18 to 21 April) then did duty in shelters as also employed for a few days in generally capturing guns (from 18 to 21 April) then did duty in shelters as A.D.S.S./Forms/C.2118. 3353 Wt.W.3544/454 700,000 5/15 D.D.&L. ROEUX and were afterwards commanded for the first week 26.4.17 under orders of 2 Guards Div Art (attach d n CHEMICAL works dangerous comforts. That we attached to the Battle of (2.25+2.5 Bde F.A.) on they did under orders of 2 Guards Div Art and now still (attach d in CHEMICAL Works dangerous comforts. That were ordered to the Battle of ATHIES.	

Vol 10

CONFIDENTIAL
No 71 (A)
HIGHLAND
DIVISION.

War Diary.

From 1st May 1917 to 31st May 1917

51st Division T. M. Batteries

WAR DIARY
or
INTELLIGENCE SUMMARY.
(Erase heading not required.)

Army Form C. 2118.

Place	Date	Hour	Summary of Events and Information	Remarks and references to Appendices
In the field	1.5.17 to 31.5.17		During the whole month, officers and men of 51st Div. T.M. Batteries were attached to the field artillery of our division (255 + 256 Brigades R.F.A). They assisted in all the fighting during the month. Casualties were as follows :— 51/X T.M. Battery had 1 man killed + 1 wounded — 51/Y 1 wounded — 51/Z 1 wounded — 51/Y 2 wounded. One officer of 51/Z T.M. Batty was wounded on 15.5.17 and has since gone home. On the 9th May, 1917 1319 Gnr. W. Chalmers of 51/X Batty was awarded the Military Medal 651 Cpl. L. G. Smith of 51/Y Batty " " " 720 Cpl. F. Henderson of 51/Z Batty " " " On the 23rd May, 1917 – 17 Heavy T.M.'s were loaded by us at ARRAS with complete stores for despatch to some other part of the line. Lieut. P.J.E. DALMAHOY was posted to 51/Z T.M. Batty with effect from 29.5.17.	J.G. Capt. J.G. Capt. J.G. Capt. J.G. Capt. J.G. Capt. J.G. Capt. J.G. Capt. J.G. Capt.

J. Gillespie Capt.
D.T.M.O. 51st Div.

CONFIDENTIAL
No 71 (A)
HIGHLAND DIVISION.

Vol XI

TRENCH MORTARS
51st Divisional Artillery

War Diary

From 1st June 1917 to 30 to June 1917.

WAR DIARY
or
INTELLIGENCE SUMMARY.
(Erase heading not required.)

Army Form C. 2118.

Place	Date	Hour	Summary of Events and Information	Remarks and references to Appendices
In the field	1.6.17 to 12.6.17		At ARRAS Officers & men attached for duty to 255 & 256th Bde.	
	13.6.17		Officers & men withdrawn from Bders	
	14.6.17		Sergt. W. Easling (No 64511) awarded V.C. for:-	
	15.6.17		most conspicuous bravery on 5th April 1917. when in charge of a Heavy T.M. Owing to a trench cartridge the breech of a discharge fell 10 yds from the hunter. Sergt Easling sprang out, lifted the one of the bombs, which had sunk the ground, uncovered the fuze & threw it in the bomb where it immediately exposed. This very gallant & prompt action undoubtedly saved the lives of the whole detachment.	
	18.6.17		T.M.s leave ARRAS in motor lorries for FREVIN CAPPELLE.	
	21.6.17		5 Officers & 40 other Ranks left FREVIN CAPPELLE for New Area, to hut lorries arriving same night also 50 other Ranks as reinforcements joined T.M. at FREVIN CAPPELLE.	
	22.6.17		Lt P.T.G. Dalmahoy goes to Hospital. Lt W. Haworth Rems of T.M. leave FREVIN CAPPELLE by train from New Area (POPERINGHE).	
	25.6.17		Captain T. Gillespie (wounded).	
	26.6.17		Captain W. Hay, Lt G.S. Robertson & Lt J.R. Todd wounded.	
	26.6.17 to 30.6.17		3 Other Ranks wounded. Officers & men employed in Ammunition Services. T.M. Practice. eighteen.	

Thos A Armstrong Lieut. RFA (TD)

CONFIDENTIAL
No 81(A)
HIGHLAND
DIVISION.

TRENCH MORTARS

WAR DIARY

From 1.7.17. — To 31.7.17.

WAR DIARY
or
INTELLIGENCE SUMMARY.
(Erase heading not required.)

Army Form C. 2118.

Place	Date	Hour	Summary of Events and Information	Remarks and references to Appendices
In the field	17.7.17		C- Nos. Tour in Bullets. Employed in making Gun emplacements on Divisional Sector (Sqr. 4x. to Sqr. 47. Reference Map ST. JULIEN Ed 6a.	N/A
	14.7.17		Working Party from BPC attached from 7/7/17 consisting of 2 offrs + 73 OR N/A Working Party from 136 A.Y. Bde Hqrs. attached from 8/7/17 consisting of 2 offrs + 73 OR. 2 Lt. E.T. Taylor + 2 Lt. D.D. Slater posted to Tn. s from D.R.E. on 7/7/17. 2 Lt. D.E. Sinclair wounded at Billet + sent to C.C.S. 13/7/17.	N/A
	15.7.17		Gun Pits Completed + firing commenced. 2 neb fired 510 rounds on Enemy Gun emplacement + one emplacement destroyed.	N/A
	17.7.17		2 neb fired 590 rds on Enemy wire + shot System with good results Enemy Retaliation fairly heavy. 6 neb Newton How fired for first time - 92 rds on enemy wire with good results.	N/A
	18.7.17		2 Lt. D.G. Sinclair died of wounds at No 10 Stationary Hospital. 2 neb fired 415 rds on enemy wire. Large gaps being made and 6 neb 102 rounds on enemy wire. Retaliation very slight.	N/A
	19.7.17		2 neb fired 435 rounds on enemy wire, new LMG wire now being cut in sector 6 neb Newton fired on enemy Trench System + dug-outs. 9.45 neb fired 55 rds on enemy Trench System. Retaliation very slight.	N/A
	20.7.17		2 neb fired 410 rds on enemy Trench System only about 30 yds of wire left in sector. Billet Kit belonging to enemy still causing 15 OR. to be killed + 28 OR to be wounded at all evacuating with the exception of 2 OR belonging to 136 A.Y. a Bde.	N/A
	21.7.17		Officers + men of 126 A.Y.a Bde unknown many direct hits being obtained 6 neb Newton fired 137 rds on dug-out alleged enemy T.M. emplacement several direct hits were obtained.	N/A
	23.7.17		2 neb fired 160 rds on remaining enemy wire. 9.45 neb fired 45 rds on enemy trench system	N/A
	23.7.17		2 neb fired 114 rds on enemy front system. 9.45 neb fired 25 rds on enemy trench system. Lt. H.H. Hay returned from Hospital + to be tempy fully Limd. to be O.C. on 31/7/17. Lt. T.H. Armstrong transfd. D.C. 51/V T.M.B.	N/A
	24.7.17		2 neb fired 84 rds on enemy Rail System. 9.45 neb fired 50 rds on enemy Trench System.	N/A
	25.7.17		2 neb fired this fairly heavy. Lt. of Saul Lane. 6 neb Newton fired 50 rds on enemy Trench System 3 neb fired 40 rds on enemy Trench System and fair nil heavy 9.45 neb fired 35 rds on enemy Trench System before for will. 2 Lt. E.E. Page + 2 Lt. R.H. Riff reinforcements.	N/A

Army Form C. 2118.

WAR DIARY
or
INTELLIGENCE SUMMARY.
(Erase heading not required.)

Instructions regarding War Diaries and Intelligence Summaries are contained in F.S. Regs., Part II. and the Staff Manual respectively. Title pages will be prepared in manuscript.

Place	Date	Hour	Summary of Events and Information	Remarks and references to Appendices
White Label	28.7.17	9.45	m.b. T.M. fired 42 rounds on enemy trench Stevin large explosion was observed, suspected enemy T.M. Amm. Dump.	N/A
	29.7.17	9.45	m.b. T.M. fired 30 rds on enemy Trench system	N/A
	28.7.17	2. m.b	T.M. 's fired 200 rds on enemy from system	N/A
		9.45	T.M. fired 26 rds on enemy Trench System	N/A
	29.7.17	9.45	T.M. fired 20 rds on enemy Trench	N/A
	30.7.17		O.P. attached from B.S.E. returned to B.H.Q.	
	31.7.17		The attack men of T.M.S employed at Stretcher Bearing. Evacuating Prisoners in advanced Dunmail Cyss bring up down from Batalian Prisoners of War to the advanced Cage. ~ on Canal Bank on Skiagyrot Post.	N/A

Casualties in action.

X/51 - N/L
Y/51 - 1 O.R Wounded

X/51 - 3 O.R wounded
Y/51 - 2 O.R wounded

Wm Hop Capt.
D.T.M.O.
51st Division

Vol 13

51st T.A. TRENCH MORTARS

War Diary

From 1.8.17. to. 31.8.17.

Army Form C. 2118.

WAR DIARY
or
INTELLIGENCE SUMMARY

(Erase heading not required.)

Place	Date	Hour	Summary of Events and Information	Remarks and references to Appendices
In the Field	1/8/17 to 4/8/17		At TROIS TOURS in Billets. Officers & men of the Try's employed in Kreveler Bearing, Guarding Prisoners in Advanced Cage, Bringing down from Battalion escort Prisoners of War to the Advanced Cage & on Canal Bank on Chaggler Post.	
	5/8/17		75% of Personnel sent to 18 pdr. & 4.5 Batteries to assist same.	
	6/8/17		From 12 noon, under 11 K. D.A. for administration & tactical purposes.	
	13/8/17 to 31/8/17		50% of Personnel sent to 18 pdr. & 4.5 Batteries returned for the purpose of working on an Ammn. Dump.	
	30/8/17		Under our own Division for administration & tactical purposes.	

N.M.Armstrong. Capt.
51st a/D.T.M.O.

CONFIDENTIAL
No 81 (A)
HIGHLAND DIVISION.

W.D. 14

War Diary

from 1st Sept 1917 to 30th Sept 1917.

of

51 Div. Artillery Trench Mortar Batteries

Army Form C. 2118.

WAR DIARY
or
INTELLIGENCE SUMMARY.
(Erase heading not required.)

Instructions regarding War Diaries and Intelligence Summaries are contained in F.S. Regs., Part II. and the Staff Manual respectively. Title pages will be prepared in manuscript.

Reference Map. POPERINGHE

Place	Date	Hour	Summary of Events and Information	Remarks and references to Appendices
38.a.	13/9/17		At TROIS TOURS - H.Q. Bayencourt	W.H.
	14/9/17		About 40 of Personnel employed each 18 pdr + 4.5 Bayencour.	W.H.
	15/9/17		One 6 in. Newton put in action & fired 24 rounds on Kearsarge Trench + Pheasant Farm.	W.H.
	16/9/17		6 in. Newton fired 210 rounds on Pheasant Trench + Blockhouses behind.	W.H.
	19/9/17		All Personnel withdrawn from Field Batteries	W.H.
	20/9/17		The Attack. T.M. Personnel employed in Stretcher Bearing. Guarding Prisoners in Advanced Cage. Bringing down from Battalion	W.H.
	22/9/17		Escorts Prisoners of War to the advanced Cage & on Stragg.Posts	W.H.
	24/9/17		All T.M. Personnel to report to 18 pdr & 4.5 Batteries for duty. Same to 2 Division.	W.H.
	26/9/17		6 in. Newton to be taken forward & fired on enemy's new positions.	W.H.
	29/9/17		All Personnel withdrawn from Field Batteries to work Mortar in the line. carrying of Amm. enroling extra work.	W.H.
	30/9/17		6 men fired 50 rds on CHURCH TRENCH. (V.25a)	W.H.

Wm Hoy Capt

D.T.M.O. 51st Divn

Vol 15

CONFIDENTIAL
No. 21 (A)
HIGHLAND
DIVISION.

War Diary

from 1/10/17 to 31/10/17

of

51st (H) Div. Trench Mortar Batteries

WAR DIARY
or
INTELLIGENCE SUMMARY.
(Erase heading not required.)

Army Form C. 2118.

Place	Date	Hour	Summary of Events and Information	Remarks and references to Appendices
In field	1.10.17		At Billets at TROIS TOURS. Personnel in the line with 18th Bat. & H.S. Batteries	
	11.10.17			
	12.10.17		All personnel withdrawn from Field Batteries pending move	
			for TROIS TOURS. in Motor Buses for NEW AREA.	
	13.10.17		Arrived at BOURG BREQUERECQUE H.Q.M. & detachment proceeded up to the line the same	
			day to take over from 50th Division.	
	14.10.17		50th Div T.M.B. withdrawn from the line.	
	15.10.17		2 med fired 70 rounds & 9.45 mor 16 rounds	
	16.10.17		2 med fired 83 rounds 3 9.45 mor 14 rounds	
	17.10.17		2 med fired 78 rounds & 9.45 mor 14 rounds. Enemy retaliation very heavy on 9.45 med Posn	
			Bow Pit.	
	18.10.17		2 med fired 80 rounds & 9.45 mor 24 rounds	
	19.10.17		2 med fired 90 rounds & 9.45 mor 50 rounds	
			3 (6 mor) Guns now in action.	
	20.10.17		2 med fired 60 rounds, 6 mor 46 and 9.45 mor 20 rounds, retaliation on the heavy mortar Pos	
			again very heavy.	
	21.10.17		2 med fired 33, 6 med 45, & 9.45 med 18 rounds. The crew of 6 Pdr 9.45 mor was to no firing 9.45	
	22.10.17		2 med fired 30 and 6 med 40 rounds	
	23.10.17		2 med fired 40, 6 med 20 rounds	
	24.10.17		2 med fired 78 rounds	
	25.10.17		2 med fired 80 and 6 med 10 rounds	
	26.10.17		Retaliation 9.45 mor withdrawn & fired 15 rounds, 2 med 69 — the long 9.45 mor 16	
	27.10.17		2 men moved from ancient Position to new position.	
			2 med fired 66 rounds, 6 med 4 & 9.45 mor 12. 2 new 6 med guns drawn from	
	28.10.17		Ordnance to-day.	
	29.10.17		2 med fired 90 rounds and 9.45 mor 10 rounds	
			2 med fired 93 rounds and 9.45 mor 11 rounds. Pechum Batteries from to-day are firing	
			as well as the enemy wire.	
	30.10.17		2 med fired 53, 6 med 47 and 9.45 mor 12 rds 18 rounds	
	31.10.17		2 med fired 86, 6 med 30 on a 9.45. 10 - 9.45 long places a new position have been closing to evade	
			2 new guns are being sent to 2 med Batteries. Position have been closing to evade	
			Enemy are long guns in pl. 6 Pdr wounded	
			Total Casualties	

W. H. J. Capt.
D.T.M.O. 51st Division

CONFIDENTIAL
No 21 A
HIGHLAND DIVISION.

9/11/16

Diary

From 1/11/17 to 20/11/17

51 Div. Arty. Trench Mortar Batts.

WAR DIARY
or
INTELLIGENCE SUMMARY.

(Erase heading not required.)

Army Form C. 2118.

Ref Sheet 57c Ed 2

Place	Date	Hour	Summary of Events and Information	Remarks and references to Appendices
In the Field	1/4/17 to 10/5/17		At Buller's at BOIRY BECQUERELLE. Detachment at Rosieres in the Line firing 6 m.b.s, 2 m.b.s and 9.45 mes Mortars.	A44
	11/5/17 to 18/5/17		From BOIRY BECQUERELLE to METZ. All Personnel with the exception of one detachment assisting Field Batteries to get up Ammunition to GUEMAPPE. One detachment placing one 9.45 met Mortar in position in FRESQUIERES.	A44 A44
	19/5/17		9.45" Mortar ready for action	
	20/5/17		The attack. 9.45 met fired 15 rds during Bombardment. All Personnel now quartered in Station Bearing Stragglers Post, Gravel on Pironnel of Nai Edge and escorting Prisoners of War to Edge, and continued borne duties for 3 days	A44 A44 A44
	23/5/17		Officer & 10 O'Ranks to Ammunition Dumps at FRESQUIERES	A44
	24/5/17		All Personnel moved to FRESQUIERES to work on Dumps.	A44
	25/5/17		All Personnel with the exception of 10 O'Ranks return to Camp behind METZ. (Q.25.a.7.4.)	A44
	30/5/17		From Camp behind METZ to Camp by NEUVILLE BOURJONVAL (Page 15.m.o) All Personnel now at the disposal of the R.R.E. and away doing slight dumps.	A44 A44

Wm Hop Capt.
54 D.T.M.O.

CONFIDENTIAL
No 21(A)
HIGHLAND
DIVISION.

Vol 17

War Diary.

From 1/12/17 To 31/12/17

51st (H) Div: T.M. Batteries

Army Form C. 2118.

WAR DIARY
or
INTELLIGENCE SUMMARY.

(Erase heading not required.)

Reference Sheet 57 e.

Instructions regarding War Diaries and Intelligence Summaries are contained in F. S. Regs., Part II. and the Staff Manual respectively. Title pages will be prepared in manuscript.

Place	Date	Hour	Summary of Events and Information	Remarks and references to Appendices
In the Field	1/2/17		At Billets "DUFFIN CAMP" on Ammunition Dumps. B29c 15.40. Personnel employed with R.E.	App 1
	2/2/17		Moved to Billets 1 mile E. of Bazenin. Personnel working for Field Batteries &c.	App 7
	5/2/17		50% of Personnel sent to T.R. School for training in 6 week courses.	App 5
	13/2/17		Personnel being withdrawn from Field Batteries as 13 Howrs are to stand now back on Divl Front.	App 13

Tho A Armstrong Capt
for 51/D.F.M.C.

Vol 18

Confidential
War Diary
From 1.1.18   To 31.1.18
of
51st Div. Artillery T.M. Batteries

WAR DIARY or INTELLIGENCE SUMMARY

Army Form C. 2118.

Reference Map 57c

Place	Date	Hour	Summary of Events and Information	Remarks and references to Appendices
In the Field	1/1/18 to 5/1/18		In Billets on Bapaume - Beronne Rd 1 mile E of Bapaume. 50% of Personnel return from T.T. School & 15% leave for training in 6 in. Newton Mortar. Personnel employed continuing Beds for 12 - 6 in. Newton Mortars & also practising portions for same	
	6/1/18 to 20/1/18		Moved to new Billets 17.11/2 cross Cap.P. I.36.b 53.19. Another 6 portions (Leperouse Portions) chosen & marked out. Considering portions & getting up ammunition.	
	21/1/18 22/1/18 23/1/18 to 31/1/18		Relieved by the 6 F. Div. & more back to Bapaume. Personnel employed shewing stables also with 6 & 25 F. Divisions' Pioneers' according to make 6 in. Newton Portions.	

Vol 19

War Diary

From 1st Feb. 1918. To 28th Feb. 1918.

of

51st (H) Div. Artillery T.M. Batteries

Army Form C. 2118.

WAR DIARY
or
INTELLIGENCE SUMMARY.
(Erase heading not required.)

Instructions regarding War Diaries and Intelligence Summaries are contained in F. S. Regs., Part II. and the Staff Manual respectively. Title pages will be prepared in manuscript.

Place	Date	Hour	Summary of Events and Information	Remarks and references to Appendices
In the field	1/3/18		Billets at Basseux.	
			Coys stationed to visit 6 K & 25 K Div. in the line.	
	5/3/18		Bn. attacked to 25 K Div. return.	
	14/3/18		Moved to Millicross Camp (I.26.6.53.9) to take over from the 6 K Div. the Division on the line astride Bapaume	
	16/3/18		Left to take over to Beaumt.	
			Holden, Intermediate positions manned by 25 K Div.	
	28/2/18		F.M. Reserve. Ammunition being taken up to the line & positions being manned.	

W.H. Olphe Capt.
O. C. M. G. 75

YA 20

War Diary
From 1/3/18 to 31/3/18
37 T.M.Bs

Army Form C. 2118

WAR DIARY
or
INTELLIGENCE SUMMARY
(Erase heading not required.)

Ref. Map
HENS 11
1/100,000

Place	Date	Hour	Summary of Events and Information	Remarks and references to Appendices
Field	13/3/18 to 20/3/18		Training & strengthening emplacements etc.	MA MA
	21/3/18		Enemy expected on sector on our left and broke through about 8 a.m. and gradually made their way over our sector from the flank. It was not until 11.15 a.m. on the 23rd that the last M.G. was abandoned. All Lewis & Vickers guns exception of 4 on the extreme right were firing whilst enemy were at very close range.	MA
	22/3/18		Orders for men who had retreated from here left FRENICOURT at 10 p.m. for OMIECOURT	MA
	23/3/18		Officers & men still returning from the Line.	MA
	23/3/18 noon		Left BOUCOURT for LE BARQUE.	MA
	24/3/18 noon		Left LE BARQUE for VRAIGNORT.	MA
	25/3/18 2am		Left MIRAUMONT for FORCEVILLE. — 9 p.m. Left FORCEVILLE for BOUSTRE.	MA
	26/3/18 10pm		Left BOUSTRE for BAVINCOURT.	MA
	28/3/18 10am		Left BAVINCOURT for LE SOUICH.	MA
	30/3/18 10am		Left LE SOUICH for GRAUNET.	MA
	31/3/18 10am		Left GRAUNET's for HAIRONS.	MA

Wm Hoyt Capt

51st Divisional Artillery

WAR DIARY

D.T.M.O.

51st DIVISIONAL ARTILLERY

APRIL 1918

Army Form C. 2118.

WAR DIARY
or
INTELLIGENCE SUMMARY.
(Erase heading not required.)

Reference No. to LENS 1/6
HAZEBROUCK 5A

Place	Date	Hour	Summary of Events and Information	Remarks and references to Appendices
ENGR.			MAYBAN'S to VERDIN ag BETHUNE.	S.J.H.
			VERDIN to BETHUNE to VEDDINGHEM	S.J.H.
			VEDDINGHEM to CAUCHY FARM.	S.J.H.
			CAUCHY FARM to HQ FUSILIERS.	S.J.H.
			HQ FUSILIERS to HQ COYS ROCK WORKS	S.J.H.
			HQ COYS ROCK WORKS to HQ FUSILIERS	S.J.H.
			Visits at LA FERRIERE. Two 6" men wounded	S.J.H.
			[illegible] on CROSSINS & BAN on COSSYN — ROAD	
			Visit ST FLORIS. [illegible] under SH 5H front line	S.J.H.
			[illegible] [illegible] RECCES American 8 Canadian [illegible]	S.J.H.
			[illegible] RECCES RA. GH SH [illegible] Cross Roads	
			to [illegible] under 5H [illegible]	
			Out 9.45 on Recce Recce to HQ Divisional & with Brigade R.A.	
			Re Conf Roles 146 Bde under 57th Div.	
			Reconnaissance with information required from appointment for King	
			to forward to Corps RA. forces Tg. as no 9mm notices.	
			S.S. at Special Report	

G.J. Hutchison Capt R.A.
S/L D.T.O

War Diary WL 22
of
51st Div. Arty T M Batts
for May, 1918

WAR DIARY
or
INTELLIGENCE SUMMARY
(Erase heading not required.)

Army Form C. 2118

Place	Date	Hour	Summary of Events and Information	Remarks and references to Appendices
Field	1/5/18		In Billets at 4A. PIERREBRE. with contact in the Line at ST FLORIS and CARVIN FARM. Firing 60/70 rounds per day from Guns at ST FLORIS & Guns at CARVIN FARM in reply for S.O.S. Under 16th Divl. Artillery for tactical purposes & administrative.	WD
	3/5/18			WD
	2/5/18		Preparing Defensive Positions behind the Line, that being done by personnel at Billets.	WD
	29/5/18		Also contact kept over in one or two minor enterprises carried out by the Infantry in the Line.	WD
	2/5/18		Relieved by the 61st Divl. Trench Mortar & men back to Guchy-au-Bois.1pdr + 30 9/Bombs went to the H.Q.D.T.M.O. as a working party.	WD
	3/5/18		Every available man to report to Corps Heavy Artillery signals on the Line as a working party. H.Q. & remain at Guchy-au-Bois.	WD

W.M.Elay Capt.
51/D.T.M.O

Confidential
—
War Diary
of
51st Div. Art. T.M Batteries
for June, 1918.

WAR DIARY
or
INTELLIGENCE SUMMARY
(Erase heading not required.)

Army Form C. 2118

No. Mass sheets 51b/NW&SW 51c.

Place	Date	Hour	Summary of Events and Information	Remarks and references to Appendices
France	1/6/18		H.Q. at AUCHY-au-BOIS, every available man in the line on Coys Fatigues.	S.J.H.
	4/5/6/18		Orders to move to CAMBLAIN-LE-ABBE. At 6hrs we move to CAMBLAIN-LE-ABBE. withdrawn from line, 5 P.M. we move to Motor Transport.	S.J.H.
	6/7/8/18		Personnel undergoing training at Billets.	S.J.H.
	11/6/18		Orders to move to the line. On the 18 P. we move in Motor Lorries & relieve the 5 P. Dev. T. R. Rear Billets & H.Q. at B.30.d.20.10. Y. Battery move from CAMBLAIN-LE-ABBE to the line over 13 - 6 men per non commd rank morning.	S.J.H.
	19/6/18 26/6/18		45 rounds fired, enemy very quiet Orders received to move 51/D D.A. defence with New Divisions in accordance with Somme	S.J.H.
	21/6/18 30/6/18		Shelling on New T.M. Emplacement etc. a/ S.J Hutchison. Co. 51/D T.M.B.O.	S.J.H.

Divisional Artillery

51st (Highland) Division

51st TRENCH MORTAR BATTERY

JULY 1918.

WAR DIARY
or
INTELLIGENCE SUMMARY

Army Form C. 2118

(Erase heading not required.)

Instructions regarding War Diaries and Intelligence Summaries are contained in F. S. Regs., Part II. and the Staff Manual respectively. Title Pages will be prepared in manuscript.

Place	Date	Hour	Summary of Events and Information	Remarks and references to Appendices
Field	12/7/18		Rehearsing new scheme in accordance with Divisional Scheme on Sw.d. Front at BAVUOEL (XV ARMY)	W.D.
	13/7/18		Lectures at Ammunition Point. These Lectures are to keep the enemy and thing from obtain Lectures	W.D.
	14/7/18		Sent for information	
			Relieved by the H.Q. Canadian T.M.S.	
	15/7/18		Left CLEUSE for TURQUES. From there entrained for PONT-SUR-SEINE	
	16/7/18 night of /17/18		Arrived at PONT-SUR-SEINE. Travelled from there to PERRY arriving at midnight of the 17/7/18.	W.D.
			30 of tanks go to meet in GERMAINE Ammunition Dump.	
			20 of tanks on 51st D.A.C. Ammunition Dump.	
			35 of tanks moved to H.Q. 51st D.A.C. went to headquarters under orders pending movement to go into action.	W.D.
	23/7/18		5/th of tanks of the above 35 are sent for duty with	
			the 1st + 2 Section D.A.C., H.Q. D.T.M.O. units H.Q. D.A.C.	
			3 front Tanks remain behind in the Line.	
	30/7/18		30 of Tanks at GEORGIE Dumps. Sent to 6/256 Bde T.M.B. for Duty at the Baby.	
	31/7/18		Received heavy casualties of NAN-SUN after advance v all O.R.'s with the exception of 6/12 a+T.I.Sect. return to Lines on 31st Reading more.	W.D.

Vol 25

War Diary

from 1st Aug. 1918 to 31st Aug. 1918.

of 51st Div. J.M. Batts

WAR DIARY or INTELLIGENCE SUMMARY

Army Form C. 2118.

Place	Date	Hour	Summary of Events and Information	Remarks and references to Appendices
Field	18/8		51st T.M. Battery entrained for New Area. 3/51 from EPERNAY. 1/51 Entrain at AVIZES +	
	21/8/18		Detrained at CALONNE + thence by Motor Lorry to FREVIN CAPELLE where Brief training was undergone until summoned from the Line on 14th inst.	
	14/8/18		The Battery complete, moved to ANZIN to take over from Division on the Line but on arrival there orders were cancelled + we returned to FREVIN CAPELLE.	
	16/8		We again moved to the Line taking up H.Q. at ECURIE + relieved the 57th Division from the Line. 52nd T.M.B. were	
	25/6/18		attacked for tactical purposes. About 20 rounds per day were fired on enemy were "dug-outs" also was being carried to the Reserve + Reserve Communication to constd. with new received from 51st D.A.	
	26/6/18		An attack was made by the Canadians who were on our Left the previous Bombardment in which the mortars fired 816 rounds.	
	27/8/18		H.Q. moved forward to R79A/2 + all ACTIVE Guns were out of range at the enemy had withdrawn sight. On account however from above mentioned attack. Four Mortars were taken in action to fire on DELSOR WOOD but when here were ready for action the enemy had withdrawn. Here Mortars stayed in Defensive Position on the Ruf Bank	

51/S.L Malley
O.C.
51st D.T.M.B

No 26

War Diary

From 1st Sept. 1918 to 30th Sept 1918.

51 T.M.B.

Army Form C. 2118

WAR DIARY
or
INTELLIGENCE SUMMARY
(Erase heading not required.) 51st R.A. Louch Mortar Batteries

Instructions regarding War Diaries and Intelligence Summaries are contained in F. S. Regs., Part II. and the Staff Manual respectively. Title Pages will be prepared in manuscript.

Place	Date	Hour	Summary of Events and Information	Remarks and references to Appendices
Field	1/9/18 to 12/9/18		Personnel of both batteries in the line preparing & visiting infantry positions on Divisional Sector.	WD
	13/9/18 to.		Relieved in the line by 49th Divisional T.M's and moved to FREVIN CAPELLE by motor lorry. In billets at FREVIN CAPELLE personnel underwent training. Experiments made with 6" T.M. mounted on Lotis Lorry, also 6" T.M. mounted on revolving bed both experiments proved very successful the shooting in both cases being accurate.	WD
	23/9/18 23/9/18 to. 30/9/18.		Moved from FREVIN CAPELLE by Motor lorry & relieved 49th Divl T.M. Batteries. 50% personnel of each battery in the line manning infantry guns. Remainder of personnel in war billets at H.T.a.1.2. Reorganising being mentioned about taken over by Army T.M. School for further instruments.	WD

30.9.18.

51st. D.T.M.B.

WSley Capt.

Vol 27

War Diary
from 1st Oct to 31st Oct 1918
51st F.R. Battn.

WAR DIARY
INTELLIGENCE SUMMARY

Army Form C. 2118

Western Front

Instructions regarding War Diaries and Intelligence Summaries are contained in F.S. Regs., Part II. and the Staff Manual respectively. Title Pages will be prepared in manuscript.

Place	Date	Hour	Summary of Events and Information	Remarks and references to Appendices
France	1/10/18		In the line near FOUEY, & ARRAS.	
	2/10/18			
	3/10/18		Relieved by the 8th Bn. L.N.F. - Proceeded by motor lorry to ANNESLES-DUISANS & remained here in training until the	
			6th Oct. 1918.	
	6/10/18		Proceeded by motor lorry to BOURLON & 39th Div. Ex. for tactical purposes. We took over the CANADIAN & and about the village of ST OLLE. Communion was taken up in readiness for pending bombardment.	
	8/10/18		From 3G trench in conjunction with attack.	
	9/10/18		We moved to ST OLLE. Guns etc went straight to the firing line here	
	11/10/18		We moved to ESCORDOEUVRES - From here we bivouaced of the & Amm Lumps.	
	13/10/18		were employed early at B&E Amm Lumps.	
	17/10/18		We moved to NAUISSE-SN-ESCOUT.	
	20/10/18		Personnel still employed on Amm Dumps & several officers	
	31/10/18		attached to R.F.A. Brigades.	

2882

153 TRENCH MORTAR BATTERY.
No. T.M. 25.
Date 6/11/18

153rd Trench Mortar Battery.

Narrative of Operations – Period 11/12 Octr. – 28/29 Octr.

Ref. Map 1/100,000 VALENCIENNES

The 153rd Inf. Bde. being Bde. in Divn Reserve followed up the 152nd and 154th Bdes. from night 11/12 Octr. until relieving 154th Inf Bde in the line on night 14/15 Octr.

Ref. Map 51ᵃ S.W.

In accordance with Bde. Order No 348 of 14th Octr. the 153rd T.M. Bty. relieved the 154 T.M. Bty. in the left subsector of the Divn. sector in the afternoon of 14th Octr. Dispositions taken over were as follows:-

Batty. Hqrs. at Iwuy N.36.c.3.0 with 4 guns in Bde. Reserve.
Two guns attached to right Btn (6th A.&S.Hrs) in position at O.13.b.8.0
Two guns attached to left Btn (7th R.Hrs) in position at railway at N.18.b.2.0.

All four forward guns were emplaced having 3 base-beds per gun permitting fire to bear on any flank if required. Guns were not laid on any particular target but could be brought into action at a moment's notice.

Officers i/c of these guns kept in close liaison with respective Btn Commanders and reported to them daily.

Guns remained in a/m. position until the forenoon of 17th Octr. when owing to heavy casualties, they were withdrawn to more suitable positions in rear. Right two guns were emplaced at O.25.a.8.8. and left two guns were emplaced at N.24.a.2.2. These positions were found more suitable as guns were now along with counter-attack Coy of each Btn.

During the period guns were in a/m positions from 14th Octr. until afternoon of 19th Octr. over 50 rounds of Stokes ammunition was expended at hostile aeroplanes with good effect.

Battery Hqrs. moved from their position at N.36.c.3.0. on the morning of 18th Octr. to N.35.b.2.1. This move took place so as to remain in close touch with Bde. Hqrs. who had also moved.

On

2.

On the afternoon of 19th Oct. word was received that the enemy were retiring opposite our front and that patrols had been pushed forward. On receipt of this message limbers were immediately sent from Batty. Hdqrs. - where they had been standing ready overnight, - to join each pair of guns, one with the right B⁺ʳ (6ᵗʰ A.&S. Hʳs) and one with the left B⁺ʳ (7ᵗʰ R.Hʳs) The captured German T.M. was detailed to accompany the right B⁺ʳ (6ᵗʰ A.&S. Hʳs)

Ref. Map. 51ᴬ N.E.

At the beginning of the advance on the 19ᵗʰ Oct. guns remained with and moved along with respective B⁺ᵗⁿˢ until their Headqrs. were established at T.27.b.3.3.

Ref. Map. 51ᴬ S.W.

Meanwhile Batty. Hdqrs. kept touch with Bde. and moved along with them establishing Batty. Hqrs. at N.6.b.60.75. at 01.00hrs. on 20ᵗʰ Oct.

Ref. Map. 51ᴬ N.E.

The guns with the right Btn. on reaching T.27.b.3.3. received word that the right flank of the B⁺ʳ was not protected. They immediately moved forward, 2 Stokes guns and the captured German T.M. and took up position at T.14.c.20.80. covering likely targets - 2 Stokes guns laid on high ground S. of Railway and German T.M. on Bolt Factory at T.15.c.4.3. The one limber remaining in close vicinity till the time. It was unnecessary to fire as no enemy attack developed. Guns remained in above stated positions until 154ᵗʰ Brigade captured THIANT and they then withdrew to DOUCHY and rejoined Batty. Hdqrs. which had moved from N.6.b.60.75 to DOUCHY. I.22.b.20.20 on night 20/21 Oct.

Ref. Map. 51ᴬ N.W.

The guns with left B⁺ʳ (7ᵗʰ R.Hʳs) on reaching T.27.b.3.3. received orders from B⁺ʳ Commander to move forward to left Coy Hqrs. which were then at I.11.b.3.3. The guns moved forward to farm I.12.a.45.55. and were emplaced there; one gun covering approach along Canal Bank and other gun laid on the Distillery at I.12.b.40.85. The guns remained in this forward position until orders were received for them to report back at Battery Hdqrs in Douchy.

DOUGHY - I.22.b.20.22. Billets were found for the whole Battery in close vicinity to Batty. Hdqrs. and the night 21/22 Oct: was spent there.

On afternoon of 22nd Oct: in accordance with Bde. Order No 356 of 22nd Oct: the 153rd T.M. Bty. relieved the 154th T.M. Bty. in billets in NOYELLES-SUR-SELLE with Batty. Hdqrs at I.34.b.60.65. The night of 22/23 Oct: was spent here.

Ref Map 51A NE

In accordance with Bde. Order No 357 of 23rd Oct: 1 Stokes T.M. was detailed to go with right Btn (6th R.Hrs) for operation, and 1 Stokes T.M plus captured German T.M. to go with left Btn for operation.

Guns moved on ½ limber to respective Btn Headqrs. on afternoon of 23rd Oct: and Bty. Headqrs. moved forward and a joint Headqrs. was established with left Btn (7th R.Hrs) at BOLT FACTORY - J.15.c.45.30.

Only 1 Gun (Stokes) was taken with each Btn owing to the difficulty in crossing the RIVER ESCAILLON for a limber. Personnel was sufficient for 1 Stokes T.M. and 1 German T.M. to move forward of river if necessary with each Btn. This however, left no personnel for the four guns in reserve at Bty. Headqrs.

The Stokes T.M. attached to right Btn (6th R.Hrs) moved along with Btn Headqrs. to J.31.d.80.70. where they remained throughout the operation as no suitable target for Stokes T.M. to engage presented itself. At 19.00 hrs. gun and personnel received orders to report at Batty. Headqrs. at BOLT FACTORY where they were billeted.

The captured German T.M. with left Btn (7th R.Hrs) was emplaced at J.15.d.10.20. and took part in initial barrage firing on known M.G's and T.M's in cemetery at J.22.a.95.45. 100 rounds were expended.

1 Stokes Mortar attached to left Btn (7th R.Hrs) advanced with 'A' Coy of this Btn to J.18.c.20. Coy Headqrs were established here and gun was emplaced to protect right flank of village of MAING, which was exposed. The gun remained in this position during night 24/25 Oct:

The personnel of German T.M. were meanwhile standing by at Bty. Headqrs. and at 11.00 hrs a German L.T.M was reported to have been captured near

/cemetery

4.

cemetery. Gun teams advanced and got this T.M. complete with ammunition emplaced near house at J.23.a.30.60. This gun was immediately turned round and fired on M.Gs in Sunken Roads south of MAING which were giving considerable trouble to Rt Btn. Gun was then taken forward during the day and by 19.30hrs was emplaced at J.18.c.2.0. covering sunken road at J.19.b.1.9. Gun remained in this position during night 24/25 Octr. Officer i/c. of these guns - the Stokes and the German T.M. - took up his Hqrs. at the forward report centre at J.18.C.2.0. and was able to keep in close liason with the Btn Commander.

On the night 24/25 Octr the 153rd Bde was relieved in the right Sub-sector of the Divl. Front by the 152nd Inf Bde and the 7th R.Hs. were relieved in the left sub-sector by the 6th A.&S.Hs. The 6th A.&S.Hs. took over the report centre established at J.18.C.2.0.

On 25th Octr the Stokes T.M. and German T.M. then came under orders of 6th A.&S.Hs. The Officer i/c remaining at the report centre keeping in touch with Btn Headqrs. at the BOLT FACTORY. The attack for the 6th A.&S.Hs. opened at 07.00hrs. The German T.M. opened fire from its position at J.18.C.2.0. at this hour on the sunken road at J.19.b.1.9. which it had been covering during the night. Hostile M.G. fire was reported to be coming from here. 40 rounds were fired and M.Gs gave no further trouble. The Stokes T.M. advanced behind the attacking waves and rendered valuable assistance firing from K.13.a.2.3. on MG firing from K.10.C.8.9. 40 rounds were expended on this target with very good effect. A M.G with 2 dead men beside it were afterwards found at a/m position. After shoot infantry were then able to continue their advance. The Stokes gun then returned to position with German T.M. as all ammunition had been expended. Further supply of ammunition was received by limber at J.18.C.2.0. at 4.00hrs on 25th Octr.

Guns/

5

Guns were not required again for that day, so were kept in defensive position at J.18.c.2.0.

On night 25/26th Oct. the 6th R.Hs. relieved the 6th A.&S.Hs. and 1 Stokes Mortar came under orders of O.C. 6th R.Hs. Very heavy casualties were suffered on 25th Oct. and personnel was only sufficient to complete one Stokes gun with carrying party.

At 08.00hrs on 26th Oct. the Stokes Gun and team moved to the forward Report Centre of the 6th R.Hs. at K.13.a.10.25. Officer i/c was able to keep in touch with B.n Comdr. through the report centre and so would be able to notify him should any of the forward coys - who knew of his position - be held up and require T.M. assistance.

A German T.M. was captured at K.13.b.60.30. Personnel of Stokes T.M. leaving their gun and ammunition at report centre, moved forward to man this mortar. It was found to be in good condition and was therefore trained in direction of Mt. HOUY. 80 rounds of ammunition were beside the mortar (40 rounds were fired on M.Gs. which were causing casualties to our Infantry - these were successfully silenced). At 17.30hrs. when a counter-attack was expected the German T.M. was firmly emplaced and gun-team were standing by ready to open fire on first sign of attack. The personnel of this team not only kept their gun ready for action but rendered valuable assistance in getting some of our Infantry who had become dislodged from their positions, owing to the intense bombardment restored to their original line. This gun team remained with the captured German T.M. until 07.30hrs. on 27th Oct. when the 6th R.Hs. were relieved by a B.n of the 154th Bde. Team then returned to billets in HAULCHIN

Bde/

6

Bde. remained in billets in HAULCHIN until 29th Oct. when they returned to DOUCHY.

6/11/18.

Archibald CAPT.
COMMANDING 153 T.M.B.

STA MT 87
28
51 D TM 863

War
Diary
from 1st Nov. to 30th Nov. 1916

Army Form C. 2118

WAR DIARY
or
INTELLIGENCE SUMMARY
(Erase heading not required.)

Place	Date	Hour	Summary of Events and Information	Remarks and references to Appendices
Field	1/11/18 to 30/11/18		4 Offrs & men attached to Bder. R.F.A., 29C. & Ammunition Dumps until the 11th November 1918. after which date they were returned & then distributed throughout Bde Artl. withdrawn, resumed from 5/16 D.R.	

MDay
Cap[t]
5/ D.T.M. ..